(Your picture goes here.
Any snapshot, formal portrait,
or self-portrait will do.)

YOUR SIGNATURE:

_____

DATE:

_____

THE BOOK OF ME

A DO-IT-YOURSELF MEMOIR

NANNETTE STONE

PETER PAUPER PRESS, INC.
WHITE PLAINS, NEW YORK

FOR JACK GITTO,
MAY LIFE BRING YOU AN ENDLESS SUPPLY
OF LOVE AND THRILLING SURPRISES.

PETER PAUPER PRESS
Fine Books and Gifts Since 1928

OUR COMPANY

In 1928, at the age of twenty-two, Peter Beilenson began printing books on a small press in the basement of his parents' home in Larchmont, New York. Peter—and later, his wife, Edna—sought to create fine books that sold at "prices even a pauper could afford."

Today, still family owned and operated, Peter Pauper Press continues to honor our founders' legacy—and our customers' expectations—of beauty, quality, and value.

Designed by Margaret Rubiano

Copyright © 2017 Peter Pauper Press, Inc.
202 Mamaroneck Avenue
White Plains, NY 10601 USA
All rights reserved
ISBN 978-1-4413-2231-9
Printed in China
21 20 19 18 17 16

Visit us at www.peterpauper.com

· CONTENTS ·

· INTRODUCTION ·

Memory is the only way home.

—TERRY TEMPEST WILLIAMS

You hold in your hands an excellent means for preserving memories, discovering hidden aspects of yourself, and clarifying goals. As you record your life story, using the guided pages that follow, your mature self will get an opportunity to meet the younger you, and future generations will get an opportunity to know who you were and what your world was like. Your pen becomes your magic wand, as it expands your awareness of the present and connects the past with the future. Just keep it moving across the page and eventually it will create a stream of information as amazing as the endless flow of brightly colored silks pulled from a magician's hat.

Use the questions and suggestions in this volume as a guide, but don't be afraid to throw in some poetry, a recipe, your new diet plan, and some doodles—anything and everything that means something to you. Using a journal that gives prompts, like this one, is easier than facing a blank page, but when inspired, go ahead and write in the margins. And if you find your entries spilling onto additional pages, that's great too. Write freely without judgment, and try not to interrupt your flow to self-edit. The only thing that counts in your journal is your passion and the freedom to write what is in your heart. This is your life, your portrait, and the person you are choosing to become all rolled up into one. Be juicy.

Whether you decide to share your journal with a partner (Leo Tolstoy and his wife Sophia did) or keep it all to yourself, you will have to decide on a way to keep it safe. You could design a special code for it, or you could learn to write backwards like Leonardo da Vinci did. Or you could just keep the unabridged version of you in a locked drawer or in some other ingenious hiding place.

What should you do with the completed journal? Leave it to someone in your will with careful instructions about how long it must be kept secret? Use it to create your memoir? Or go public? Lately an increasing number of people read their most embarrassing entries at open mike nights to enthusiastic coffeehouse crowds. Still others submit their most humiliating passages for publication. On second thought, probably the best thing to do is use your journal to remind yourself of how much you've grown, to recall your personal history, and to share a life with those you love.

Remember, you don't have to be old to forget. Memories are fragile and easily muddled. Over time the details get fuzzy and even your most poignant memories can be contaminated by what you hear others say. *The Book of Me* will set the record straight and retain all the facts you need to trigger vivid recall. Because you were there.

• HINT •

Be specific whenever you can be. Precise details will add authenticity and will make your story come alive. Use both first and last names whenever possible. Your great granddaughter could have trouble figuring out that "John" is your friend from college, even though it seems quite obvious now. Try for as many exact dates, locations, addresses, brand names, and species (etc.) as possible. Say "that mist green 1950 Chevy" instead of "Dad's car," say "the old public hospital on Seventh Street that burned down in 2001," instead of "the old hospital," and "pink peonies," not "nice flowers."

Do not trust your memory; it is a net full of holes;
the most beautiful prizes slip through it.

—GEORGES DUHAMEL

THE FACTS OF LIFE

Just the facts, ma'am. All we want are the facts.

—ATTRIBUTED TO SERGEANT JOE FRIDAY IN *DRAGNET*

When you describe yourself think about giving future generations a peek at how you appear in the flesh. Try to see yourself as a stranger would, and think about what that person might know or guess about you at first glance. Practice objectivity and self-acceptance. Don't be critical. Make this an exercise in appreciating the large and small details that make you YOU.

It's true that the probability of an identical snowflake or of an identical you is about zero. You were born to look, think, and act like no other. And we're not just talking fingerprints or genetic spirals. Even if you are a monozygotic twin, you began to develop into a person noticeably different from your womb mate almost as soon as your mutual egg split into two embryos. Your individuality kicked in around the time of your conception and will continue to grow throughout your life span.

You have been naturally endowed with certain physical traits, gifts, and proclivities. But you are much more than a blueprint. You also came equipped with a natural inclination to self-actualize—that is, to grow into the person you are capable of becoming. Along with your life experience, the choices you've made have shaped your skills, habits, preferences, character, and personal style into unique you. Your mannerisms and physical appearance are shining expressions of the inherited you and the self you have chosen to be.

· AKA ·

According to the *Guinness Book of World Records* 1978 edition, the longest name used by anyone is Adolph Blaine Charles David Earl Frederick Gerald Hubert Irvin John Kenneth Lloyd Martin Nero Oliver Paul Quincy Randolph Sherman Thomas Uncas Victor William Xerxes Yancy Wolfeschlegelsteinhausenbergerdorff.

What is your full given name?

How was that name chosen?

What do you like to be called?

What are all the other names you have used? *(nicknames, religious, married, or pseudonyms)*

How did you get those names?

Have you ever been called by a name that was distasteful or hurtful? *(Explain.)*

If you could choose a different name, what would it be?

· ID-OLOGY ·

Your name ....

Current age ....

Height .... Weight ....

Eye color .... Hair color ....

Address ....

Phone ....

Email ....

Describe your physical appearance and typical behavior so that a complete stranger could pick you out of a crowd.

....

....

....

....

....

....

....

....

Do you have distinguishing features, such as a birthmark, scar, tattoo, big teeth, or a mole?

....

....

....

....

....

What signature clothes or accessories—such as tight blue jeans, a rotary pin, or a purple scarf—do you usually sport?

....

....

....

....

....

What mannerisms distinguish you? *(Would your whistle, your figures of speech, or a pen tucked over your ear give you away?)*

....

....

....

....

....

· NOTES TO SELF ·

MY LIFE:
A PERSONAL HISTORY

Memory is a way of holding on to the things you love,
the things you are, the things you never want to lose.

—KEVIN ARNOLD

This chapter is an invitation to record the unique facts of your life history, from your very beginning through the journey of childhood, adolescence, and young adulthood..

Adults can have trouble summoning up their childhood. Recollections from age three or even earlier are possible, but most of what happens in early childhood has been buried in the neurocircuitry of more recent experience. Names and events can be squeezed from your 100 billion brain cells with conscious effort, but involuntary memories, the gems that Marcel Proust said hold the true essence of the past, are spontaneous and more elusive. Fortunately you can jog them. Because intellectual memory triggers involuntary memory, poignant bits of your past will probably pop up naturally as you track down facts for your journal. But you can also use sensual experience to coax them into consciousness. Can you think of sounds, tastes, and smells associated with your past? For instance: If your mother wore Chanel No. 5, go to the perfume counter and ask for a whiff. Listen to an old recording of nursery songs. Did you ever sing "I'm a Little Teapot" or "Itsy Bitsy Spider"? Look at old photo albums and reproductions of vintage Sears catalogues. Talk to people about the old days and compare notes. Mine the gap.

· IN THE BEGINNING: MY DEBUT ·

What were you told, or what do you suspect, about your mother's pregnancy with you, the day you were born, and your first few days at home?

_____

_____

_____

_____

_____

_____

_____

_____

_____

_____

_____

_____

_____

_____

Where and when were you born? _____

How much did you weigh? _____ How long were you? _____

Were you quiet or colicky? _____

_____

MY LIFE: A PERSONAL HISTORY

What have you been told about your exploits and personality in your earliest years?

_____

_____

_____

_____

_____

_____

_____

_____

What was your first word, and its context?

_____

_____

_____

_____

When did you begin walking? Write any details you know.

_____

_____

_____

If adopted, what and when were you told about your adoption? ....

....

....

....

....

....

....

What were you told about your birth parents? ....

....

....

....

....

....

....

What do you know about the first time your parents saw you and the day they brought you home?

....

....

....

....

....

....

....

What else have you wanted to know?

What kind of home did you come into and what was the address?

What can you glean from memories or photographs about the rooms, your crib, the furniture, the wallpaper in the kitchen, or other decorations?

What kinds of stories did you hear about the reactions of siblings, grandparents, family friends, and others to your arrival?

_____

_____

_____

_____

_____

_____

_____

_____

What strikes you about the baby books, infant clothes, portraits, or other artifacts from those very early days?

_____

_____

_____

_____

_____

_____

_____

Was there a welcoming celebration? *(a bris, a baptism, a baby naming ceremony, or other family ritual for you?)* If so, give details.

....

....

....

....

....

....

Whether by design or by accident, the circumstances of your birth presented you with a very unique set of advantages and challenges. What were they?

....

....

....

....

....

....

....

....

....

....

· MY EARLY YEARS ·

What is your earliest memory?

What was a favorite book or bedtime story?

What do you remember about, or what were you told about, your learning to read?

Who babysat you, and what were they like?

Children frequently make an emotional attachment to some object that comforts them. What blankie or favorite crib doll did you use? Did it have a name?

MY LIFE: A PERSONAL HISTORY

Describe your favorite game or toy. ....

....

What toy from your past do you wish you still had? ....

....

What songs or dances or jump rope rhymes are part of your early childhood?

....

....

Do you remember the arrival of any younger siblings? Earliest interactions with older siblings?

....

....

....

....

How was your first day in nursery school or kindergarten? ....

....

....

....

What was the name of your first school and where was it? ....

....

Write about your favorite teacher.

Describe your first school chum.

What was your family's religious preference?

How often did you go to services, Sunday school, or religious training, and what was it like?

Describe how you learned to skate, swim, or ride a bicycle.

Write about any pets you had. *(What did you name them? Which ones were your favorites?)*

What was the most unusual animal you kept? *(a one-legged bird, a skunk, a squirrel?)*

Were there any imaginary friends in your life? *(Explain.)*

What is the first time you remember getting punished for something?

What was most scary to you? *(the dark, the space under your bed, your Uncle Jack, dogs, clowns?)* How did you overcome that fear?

What things that you used to enjoy no longer exist? *(candy wax lips, Fizzies, beepers, boy bands, Pac-Man, phone booths with coin slots?)*

What memories do you associate with those bygone things?

· ADOLESCENCE ·

Adolescence is awkward if not downright painful. What an ambush of physical, emotional, and social change! You could get walloped with the exhilaration of new love, a heady political argument with your parents, some peer pressure to play hooky, the wonder of a falling star, and a hideous zit on your nose all in one day. Looking good, athletic prowess, and membership in the right clique feel urgent. Those teen friendships, rejections, failures, and successes have such a profound impact on self-concept that, in a way, no one ever leaves high school entirely behind. What do you remember most about the way your body changed, the rush of hormones, the academic and social pressures? What was your relationship with your parents like during that time? As you remember the teenager you once were, be empathetic and muster the courage to be candid about this difficult time.

What were your school names and locations?

How many students were in your high school graduating class?

What about your parents seemed old-fashioned?

What rites of passage marked your coming of age? *(Did you get confirmed, have a bar/bat mitzvah, or gain a privilege that signified new status?)*

....

....

....

When and in what place were you so honored? *(Describe your experience.)*

....

....

....

....

....

....

....

....

....

....

....

....

....

When were you tempted to do something you thought was wrong, just to fit in, and what did you decide to do?

_____

_____

_____

_____

How did you handle competition?

_____

_____

_____

_____

Were you confident or fearful? *(Give examples.)*

_____

_____

_____

_____

What was it like back then to run for a school office, enter a contest, participate in a debate, or vie for something else?

_____

_____

_____

_____

MY LIFE: A PERSONAL HISTORY

What concerned you most about your appearance, and why? ....

....

Did your skin break out? ....

What remedies and cover-ups did you try? ....

....

How did you size up next to your classmates? *(Were you thinner, fatter, taller, or shorter?)*

....

....

....

Did you mature faster or more slowly than most of your friends?

....

How did you feel about your bra size or the state of your beard?

....

What clothes were in fashion? ....

....

To what lengths did you go to get the right jacket, sweater, shoes, or accessory?

....

....

....

How did you style your hair? *(Did you perm, iron, dye, or shave it?)*

....

How much did you worry about being popular?

Whom did you hang out with after school?

Who sat with you at lunch?

What was memorable about the school food?

How would you describe your group of friends?

Are you still in touch with any of them? *(Who and in what way?)*

MY LIFE: A PERSONAL HISTORY

What did your parents think of your choice of friends?

Did you have a crush on a classmate? *(Describe.)*

What about a teacher, movie star, singer, or someone else?

What kind of music did you listen to?

What songs come to mind from your teen years?

What movies do you remember seeing?

What about TV shows?

Describe your first kiss.

Describe your first date.

Did you go steady?

Describe the first time you fell in love. *(Was it reciprocated? How long did it last?)*

What pressure, either from within or from others, did you feel to engage in physical intimacy?

....

....

....

If you surrendered to those feelings, what was the experience like and how did you feel afterward?

....

....

....

....

....

Describe your first exposure to homosexuality. ....

....

....

....

....

What is the most embarrassing event, related to your physical maturation, that happened to you? Explain.)

....

....

....

....

Back then, what did you think you were going to be when you grew up?

....

....

Did you go to the prom? *(With whom? What did you wear? Did you know how to dance?)*

....

....

....

Where did you go after the prom, if anywhere? ....

....

....

....

If you didn't go to the prom, what did you do instead? ....

....

....

....

How athletic were you, and how was this manifested? ....

....

....

....

When teams were picked in gym class, were you picked first, near the beginning, in the middle, or toward the end—and how was that for you?

....

....

What school clubs, sports teams, or other organizations did you join?

....

....

What form of recognition did you receive? *(any awards or trophies?)*

....

....

What activities outside of school did you participate in? *(Describe your involvement.)*

....

....

....

What was your grade point average? ....

What is the worst test score or grade you got? ....

Describe a memorable teacher or class. ....

....

....

....

What was your best subject? ....

....

What subjects challenged you? ....

....

....

Were you expected to do well?

How did you respond to others' expectations?

How much did you worry about your future?

Getting into college?

Getting a job?

Who was the first adult you considered a friend? Describe this relationship.

What was your attitude about drugs and alcohol?

Who taught you to drive, and how?

_____

_____

What kind of car did you use to practice driving, and what did it look like?

_____

_____

Did you have access to the family car? (_What was the arrangement?_)

_____

_____

_____

Did anyone in your school have a fatal accident, serious injury, or a life threatening disease?

_____

_____

How well did you know them? Describe what happened.

_____

_____

_____

Look at your yearbook photos. If you met that kid today what would you make of him or her?

_____

_____

_____

Write a letter to yourself as a teen. What kind of person were you then? What advice or reassurance can you offer? What do you want him or her to know about the future?

· MY YOUNG ADULT YEARS ·

Between adolescence and maturity you faced some major decisions about work and love. Freud said so. You cut the apron strings and probably at least considered tying the knot. You explored the possibilities, sized yourself up, chose a career, and sought passionate love. How did those turning points shape who you are now?

What was your dream job when you were in high school?

What plans for the future had to be modified because of academic, financial, or other practical limitations?

How did this affect you?

What did you do right after high school?

What trade, vocational training, higher education, travel, military service, marriage, or other options were available to you?

If you pursued higher education, training, or the military, describe where you went and what you studied. Describe your fondest memories, and the value of the experience then and now.

How did you spend your summers?

What was your highest academic achievement?

How were you able to do that?

What teachers, bosses, or other mentors influenced you, and how?

What do you wish they had taught you in school?

What did you learn in the school of hard knocks?

Which lessons about managing money, creating a social life, and staying on track at work came easily?

When, if ever, did you spend money unwisely, bounce a check, miss something important because you overslept, or otherwise made unwise moves?

• IF THEY COULD SEE ME NOW •

Write a letter to a teacher or someone else who made an impression on you when you were young. Describe your life today. Were you encouraged by his or her support, or did you rise above his or her predictions to prove them wrong?

Describe your first real job.

What kind of employee did you make?

What did you learn about your strengths and weaknesses?

What role did your family's expectations play in your choice of occupation?

How did you embrace or rebel against those expectations?

How much of your career decision was based on a desire for a high income? A natural talent or strong intellectual interest? A wish to help people or contribute to society?

When did you leave your parental home and get your own place?

....

....

....

....

How far away did you move? ....

What was the address? ....

....

Describe the neighborhood, your furniture, your early purchases, and the way you felt about being in that first home away from home.

....

....

....

....

....

....

....

....

How did you get to work? ....

What was the first vehicle you bought? ....

MY LIFE: A PERSONAL HISTORY

What is the wildest party you ever attended, threw for yourself, or got thrown out of?

What was the biggest financial gamble you ever took?

How did it play out?

Biggest emotional risk (and outcome)?

Biggest risk to your physical safety (and outcome)?

What is the most thrilling unplanned thing that happened to you?

How did you go about meeting lovers and friends at this stage of your life?

What opportunity for money or love did you pass up? Do you ever regret it?

Describe your most romantic date.

How many romantic relationships did you have before you developed a serious interest in someone? *(Identify and describe them.)*

....

....

....

....

....

What first attracted you to a "significant other"?...

....

....

What personal characteristics, values, or interests deepened the relationship?

....

....

....

When and why did you consider yourself ready to make a commitment to a relationship?

....

....

....

....

....

MY LIFE: A PERSONAL HISTORY

· NOTES TO SELF ·

· NOTES TO SELF ·

ALL IN THE FAMILY

Family faces are magic mirrors. Looking at people who belong to us, we see the past, present, and future.

—GAIL LUMET BUCKLEY

Better than a pirate's chest, a collection of treasured memories about family is worth digging up. Any story about you and your ancestors that includes sentiment, secrets, keen observations (kind or catty), naughty behavior, or acts of kindness, becomes a priceless gift not only for your contemporaries but for many generations to come. Record them for posterity. Be generous with your details and don't hesitate to include your own opinions. Value what you have to say.

If you lack information, now may be a good time to organize a family reunion. Reminiscing often brings people closer, and it may be more fun for you to research and improve your project that way. When in doubt, leave nothing out. If cousin John always embellishes, express your skepticism in the margin, but record his story verbatim. Incorrect grammar and an occasional curse word can be considered color rather than edited out.

Take your time when it comes to memory. It is likely to surface unevenly and imperfectly. Leave blank spaces where necessary and come back to them later. A few thorough accounts can be better than pages filled with cursory answers.

ALL IN THE FAMILY

· MY FATHER ·

What is (was) your father's full name?

When and where was he born?

What did he do for a living?

What did he do for fun?

What special talents and skills did he have? *(Was he artistic, musical, athletic, a great storyteller?)*

What did you inherit from him? *(his nose, his temperament, his gait, his occupation?)*

One important thing I learned from him was:

hat I liked about him most was: ....

....

....

he biggest challenge in our relationship was: ....

....

....

he grew older he became: ....

....

here is he now? ....

only wish that he had: ....

....

....

only wish that I had: ....

....

....

· MY MOTHER ·

What is (was) your mother's maiden name?

When and where was she born?

What kind of work, if any, did she do outside the home or before she married?

What did she do for pleasure?

What were her skills and special talents?

What physical, emotional, and/or material things did you inherit from her?

What one important thing did you learn from having her as a mother?

What did you appreciate most in her?

What was the biggest challenge in your relationship?

What changed as you both grew older?

Where is she now?

I only wish that she had:

I only wish that I had:

ALL IN THE FAMILY

· MY PARENTS ·

If you were adopted, what do you know about your birth parents?

_____

_____

_____

_____

_____

What do you know about how your parents met, fell in love, popped the question, and got married?

_____

_____

_____

_____

How old were they when they married?

If you could have changed one thing about your parents what would it have been?

_____

_____

_____

_____

ALL IN THE FAMILY

What are your siblings' names and birth dates? ....

....

....

....

Where are you in the birth order? *(youngest, oldest, third out of five?)* ....

....

Would you describe your early home life as (circle one): *A Love Story, The Brady Bunch, The History of Violence, Survivor, Let's Make a Deal,* or some other movie or show? Why?

....

....

....

....

....

....

....

....

....

....

....

....

· MY MOTHER'S FAMILY ·

What were your mom's parents' names?

By what names did you call them?

When and where were they born?

What was their national heritage?

What were their occupations?

Where did they live when she was growing up?

What did your mom tell you about the kind of home life she had as a child?

Who were your mother's brothers and sisters and what were they like as children?

ALL IN THE FAMILY

How well did you get to know your maternal grandparents?

....

....

....

How much time did they spend with you when you were small? ....

....

....

How involved were they in your upbringing? ....

....

....

What do you most remember about them? ....

....

....

....

What else do you know about your maternal grandparents?

....

....

....

What about maternal great grandparents and other people in your family tree?

....

....

ALL IN THE FAMILY

· MY FATHER'S FAMILY ·

What were your dad's parents' names?

What did you call them?

When and where were they born?

What was their national heritage?

What did they do for a living?

Where did they live when your dad was growing up?

What do you know about your father's early home life and upbringing?

Who were his brothers and sisters and what were they like as children?

ALL IN THE FAMILY

How well did you get to know your paternal grandparents?

....

....

....

How much time did they spend with you when you were small?

....

....

....

How involved were they in your upbringing? ....

....

....

What do you most remember about them? ....

....

....

....

What else do you know about your paternal grandparents?

....

....

....

What about paternal great grandparents and other people in your family tree?

....

....

· FAMILY LORE ·

What family legends do you know about? *(Is anyone famous or infamous? Did someone live to be 103? How did they immigrate to this country? Did they join a wagon train or pan gold?)*

_____

_____

_____

_____

_____

_____

_____

Are there any stories, secrets, or skeletons lurking in your family closets?

_____

_____

_____

_____

_____

_____

_____

Most family trees produce some nuts. What member of your family is considered eccentric, and how?

....

....

....

....

....

....

....

....

Do you harbor any family eccentricities? *(Describe.)* ....

....

....

....

....

If you want a few more clues about your early ancestry and ethnicity, you can take a genealogical DNA test, using a cheek swab sample, with a home kit or by visiting a DNA test clinic.

ALL IN THE FAMILY

· INFLUENTIAL RELATIVES ·

What aunts, uncles, cousins, or other relatives played an important part in your life, and how?

....

....

....

....

....

....

Who were your favorites? ....

....

What made that person or persons appeal to you? ....

....

....

....

....

....

you could influence a younger relative, who would it be, and why?

....
....
....
....
....
....
....
....
....

ן what way(s) would you like to mentor, guide, or help them?

....
....
....
....
....
....
....
....

· MY CONTEMPORARY RELATIVES ·

How colorful are the branches of your family tree? Note a detail or two about each of your siblings and/or cousins. *(Was one of them freckled, a brainiac, or always hogging the phone?)*

_____

_____

_____

_____

_____

_____

_____

_____

What did family members always say about you as a child? _____

_____

_____

_____

How different is that from what they say about you as an adult? _____

_____

_____

_____

ALL IN THE FAMILY

Who in your family was always considered to be particularly:

Smart? ....

Good looking? ....

High maintenance? ....

Creative? ....

Well behaved? ....

The black sheep? ....

Mommy's or Daddy's favorite? ....

What other labels were assigned to specific family members? ....

....

....

....

How accurate or fair were they? ....

....

....

....

Did expectations seem to influence family members? ....

....

....

....

....

· SEEDS AND SAPLINGS ·

Did you choose to marry? Once, or more times? *(to whom?)*

....

....

If so, how did you meet your spouse(s) and when did you tie the knot(s)?

....

....

....

....

What is your spouse like? ....

....

....

....

In each case who proposed how, and was it a surprise?

....

....

....

....

What kind of ceremony did you have and where did it take place?

....

....

....

....

Did you go on a honeymoon? If so, describe it. ....

....

....

....

How did you decide if and when to have children? ....

....

....

What are the names and dates of birth (or adoption) of each of your children? If you have no children of your own, what stepchildren or other children are special to you?

....

....

....

What do you remember most about each child's birth and early years?

What has been most challenging about parenting each of your children?

What makes you proudest of each child?

ALL IN THE FAMILY

· NOTES TO SELF ·

ALL ABOUT ME

It has long been an axiom of mine that
the little things are infinitely the most important.

—ARTHUR CONAN DOYLE

Know thyself is ancient and classic good advice. Though the answers to "Who am I, why am I here, and where am I going?" may dodge you, clues may emerge between the lines of your responses to the prompts in this chapter. Here is the place to record the details of your life—places you've lived, work you've done, friends and neighbors you've had, personal habits you've harbored, and what your physical reality looks like. Here is the place, also, to transcribe yourself in the context of your larger world, detailing the significant historic events of your lifetime, creating a "slice of life" and a "time capsule" snapshot of your typical day.

Embrace your own version of the life you have lived. Be spontaneous. If you find it hard to be candid with yourself, you may find it easier to put mind and heart on paper while pretending to address a real or imaginary friend. Occasionally people find it freeing to write about themselves in third person. Write it all down and see what you learn from yourself.

If you feel you must edit for posterity, do so only after you have first written freely. You may decide that the exploration of your wildest episodes and secret emotions are interesting and valuable—if not squeaky clean. Maybe you'll leave it in. Then again, words and phrases that have been completely scratched out have a certain fascination too.

· OH, THE PLACES I'VE BEEN! ·

ive the addresses and describe the main residences in which you have lived.

....

....

....

....

....

....

....

raw a diagram of your bedroom.

What was special about each neighborhood you lived in, and what special features do you remember from each place? *(a tree you could see from your window, the way the kitchen smelled?)*

ALL ABOUT ME

List and describe the principal places you've visited for business or pleasure.

Describe a family vacation that stands out in your memory.

Write about a vacation you've taken by yourself.

Where would you like to travel next, and why?

· WEOLOGY—FRIENDS AND LOVERS ·

What is the first and last name of your first best friend? ....

How did you meet and become friends? ....

_____

_____

_____

_____

Who have some of your other best buddies been? ....

_____

_____

_____

_____

Do you have a best friend now? *(Explain.)* ....

_____

_____

_____

Have you been cheated by a family member, a friend, or a lover? If so, how?

....

....

....

Have you ever betrayed someone? If so, explain.

....

....

....

When did someone stick up for you or help you when you needed it?

....

....

....

How many times have you been in love? *(Describe the situations.)*

....

....

....

....

....

Were you ever the first to use the L word?

....

Describe your best overall romantic experience.

Your worst?

What was your first physically intimate experience like?

What relationships have you lost through divorce, death, or other circumstances, and what was that like?

_____

_____

_____

_____

_____

_____

_____

What have you done to recover from those losses? _____

_____

_____

_____

_____

_____

_____

_____

_____

If you have more than one child, how are your affections different for each one?

_____

_____

_____

_____

_____

How does your parenting differ from the way you were raised?

_____

_____

_____

_____

_____

In what ways do you try to be (or would you try to be) a better parent to your child than your parents were to you?

_____

_____

_____

_____

_____

it possible to be in love with more than one person at a time?

_____

_____

_____

_____

How important is it that your lover or marriage partner be:

Physically attractive? In what ways? _____

_____

Intelligent? _____

Rich? _____

Kind? _____

Helpful? _____

Have a sense of humor? _____

What else is important to you? _____

_____

_____

_____

_____

_____

_____

Did you ever choose to sever a relationship with a family member or very close friend, and why?

Did anyone ever cut you off abruptly? Explain what happened.

Do you ever consider reconciliation?

What would it take for that person to deserve your forgiveness or for you to want to let go of that resentment?

....

....

....

....

....

Who have you not forgiven? ....

....

....

....

....

....

Is there anyone with whom you have been too forgiving?

....

....

....

....

....

You agree to spend an entire year on a remote tropical island as part of a scientific study on the body's response to pure pleasure paired with a diet that includes a rare subspecies of coconut. The setting is a luxurious paradise replete with gourmet food and plenty of sunscreen. You will be paid handsomely for your participation and can expect a permanent result of perfect health. You can take up to five people with you. They too will reach a state of permanent well-being. Here's the rub. Any discord will ruin the study for everyone. Who, if anyone, gets to come with you? Who among those you love would probably be unable to fulfill the contract?

Your genie in a lamp grants you three absolutely true answers instead of wishes. If you could ask anyone anything, who are the people you'd question, and what would you want to know?

Psychologists say it takes ten items of praise to counter a single criticism. Are you careful about the way you express disapproval?

How good are you at giving praise and compliments?

How much do you care about what other people think of you?

How do you respond to negative comments?

Can you take a compliment?

Do you ever say nice things to your bathroom mirror?

· VOLUNTEERING ·

is often said, especially when it comes to community work, that twenty percent of the eople do eighty percent of the work. What's your share?

....

....

....

....

o you volunteer, have you volunteered, or will you volunteer time or money to a ommunity, religious, or local political group? Describe what you've done or will do.

....

....

....

....

....

....

....

....

....

....

....

· THE PEOPLE NEXT DOOR ·

Describe your neighbors.

Are you cordial but distant, or do you live in each other's pockets?

What makes a good neighbor?

....

....

....

....

....

Have you ever had a fight with a neighbor? *(Explain.)*

....

....

....

....

....

Ever had loud, messy, nosy, or otherwise troublesome folks living nearby? Describe the situation and how you handled it.

....

....

....

....

....

· WORKING LIFE ·

List and describe all the jobs you've had.

_____

_____

_____

_____

_____

_____

_____

_____

_____

_____

_____

What's the best job you ever had, and why?

_____

_____

_____

_____

_____

ALL ABOUT ME

What kind of work do you do now? *(Stay-at-home parents, don't skip this one.)*

Where do you work? *(Give the address.)*

What do you like and dislike about what you do?

How are you good at your job?

What are your shortcomings at work?

ALL ABOUT ME

How long is your commute? ....

List a positive and a negative aspect of your commute. ....
....

What kind of training, supervision, or continuing education do you receive?
....
....

Did you ever quit a job, and if so, what were the circumstances?
....
....
....
....

Have you ever been fired, and why? ....
....
....
....
....

What's your dream job? ....
....
....
....
....

· RESISTING A REST ·

Do you delegate tasks easily? ....

Are you ever reluctant to go on vacation? ....

Do you ever work when you should stay home sick? ....

Are your weekends filled with projects and errands or a lot of naps?

....

Is your vacation filled with activities *(sightseeing, hiking, swimming)* or a lot of time lying down?

....

Right now are you lying down? ....

Do you fall asleep easily? ....

Do you toss and turn or sleep through the night? ....

What do you think about retirement? ....

....

....

....

Would you ever take a sabbatical or a leave of absence? If not, why? If so, what would you do?

....

....

....

· NAUGHTY OR NICE—CONFESSIONS ·

What's the first naughty deed you ever committed? *(Explain.)*

What deed did you think about doing but didn't?

What have you gotten away with?

When did you get caught red-handed?

How good are you at telling lies?

you could never get caught what might you be tempted to do? ....

....

er cheated on an exam? *(Explain.)* ....

....

er hurt someone through dishonesty? ....

....

hat sort of guilt pangs do you suffer? ....

....

hat do you regret doing? ....

....

....

hat do you regret *not* doing? ....

....

....

· ACQUISITION ·

What's your shopping style?

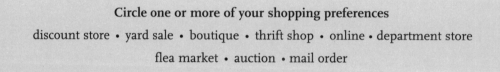

Circle one or more of your shopping preferences

discount store · yard sale · boutique · thrift shop · online · department store

flea market · auction · mail order

Do you like to browse for pleasure or inspiration?

Do you shop only for necessities?

Can you recall an impulse buy?

What is your very best all-time bargain?

When did you pay too much for something?

....

....

....

....

What do you wish you had snapped up when you had the chance?

....

....

....

What did you use only once?

....

....

....

Do you know how to sell things online?

....

....

Do you ever haggle? Are you good at it? What makes a good haggler?

....

....

....

....

· PRIZED POSSESSIONS ·

What heirlooms do you possess?

What gift do you treasure?

What is the most expensive thing you own? How much did you spend and what is it worth?

What do you keep just because you loved it in the past?

What five things (not living) would you save in a house fire, and why?

....

....

....

....

....

....

What possession(s) speaks loudest about what kind of person you are?

....

....

....

....

....

....

What do you always throw out that you should probably keep? ....

....

....

What do you wish you could own but probably never will? Why do you want it?

....

....

....

....

....

....

· MONEY MATTERS ·

> **Fiscal Scotoma**—It's not a disease. Just a common blind spot. No wonder. In our culture money is so rarely openly discussed that it has been dubbed the last taboo.

Is money the root of all evil? *(Explain your answer.)*

What did you learn about the value of money from your family?

What money issues have surfaced in your current life? In your personal relationships?

How much were you paid for your first full-time job, and in what year was that?

Are you paid what you are worth? Why or why not? What *are* you worth?

Do you pay bills on time?

Do you feel happy to be able to pay your bills or resent parting with your money?

Have you ever written "thank you" on a payment when you sent it in?

How easy is it to live within your means?

How often do you donate money and time to a charity? *(Explain.)*

How much do you usually tip a waiter?

When have you been generous?

What makes you feel stingy?

Are you a natural saver or a spender? Why do you think that is?

If you had a million extra, unallocated dollars, what would you spend it on?

· THE IMPORTANCE OF PLUMAGE ·

Both men and women often have love-hate relationships with their hair. How do you like yours?

_____

_____

_____

_____

Describe the style and draw a sketch of it. _(Is it long or short? Do you sport bangs, a bob, braids, or a bald spot? Are you all done up or do you let it all hang down?)_

_____

What dyes, perms, or false pieces have you (or would you) use? _____

_____

_____

How do you feel about the person who styles your hair? About being fawned over?

....

....

....

....

....

What was your most appallingly bad hair day? *(an extremely bad haircut, perm, or color?)*

....

....

....

....

What is the most extreme hairdo you have ever had? *(Rapunzel extensions? Mohawk? multicolored? Afro?)*

....

....

....

....

Describe the best hairstyle you ever had. ....

....

....

....

· PHYSICAL APPEARANCE ·

How important are your looks to you?

What is your best feature?

How physically attractive do you consider yourself to be?

Describe a feature that stands out to you on:

• Your best friend

• Your significant other

• Siblings

• A coworker

Have you inherited any particular family trait? *(kinky hair, a tendency to blush?)*

How do you feel about it?

ALL ABOUT ME

Describe the most drastic change you have ever made in your appearance? *(shaved off beard, had surgery, gotten tattooed, dyed your hair, gained or lost weight?)*

What effect did it have on how you felt about yourself?

How did other people respond?

Is there anything you wish you could change about your appearance?

Can you?

· CLOTHING ·

What's your pleasure? *(baggy pants, sequined gowns, cowboy hat, nothing at all?)*

....

....

....

How do different outfits you wear make you feel? ....

....

....

....

What do you like to wear most:

- At home? ....

- At work? ....

- To paint the town red? ....

- To sleep? ....

- In your wildest dreams? ....

Ever wear a uniform to school or work? ....

....

....

To what extent do clothes make the man? Or the woman?

What did (or would) you once wear to a costume party?

Is there anything you are certain you would never ever wear? *(a mask, floppy hat, thong, fur?)*

What is your signature style? *(vintage jewelry, green socks, retro eyeglass frames?)*

What's your favorite color?

Do you prefer to dress in hot pinks and neon greens, earth tones, pastels, or primary colors?

Do you wear the colors you like often?

· A MILE IN YOUR SHOES ·

What do your shoes say about you? ....

....

....

....

....

....

How many pairs of shoes do you own? ....

....

What interests do they represent? *(running shoes, golf shoes, ballet slippers, ski boots?)*

....

....

....

....

....

....

....

ifferent kinds of shoes express particular moods. What do yours *(spike-heeled slippers with feathers, psiders)* say about your varied moods?

_____

_____

_____

_____

_____

_____

Iave you kept any that hurt your feet? For what reason? _____

_____

_____

Vhat was your favorite pair of shoes of all time? _____

_____

_____

Vhat is the earliest pair of shoes you can remember wearing, and what do you recall about them?

_____

_____

_____

_____

_____

107

· SLICE OF LIFE ·

A grocery list or a peek into your refrigerator may seem mundane now, but in 100 years it's bound to be fascinating. Imagine your great-great-grandchild finding that you, like she, preferred olives stuffed with garlic rather than pimento or that in the olden days people actually shopped for their vegetables in person.

What favorite or unusual items can be found in your kitchen cabinets and refrigerator?

The drawings, photos, appointment cards, magnets, invitations, and reminder notes on your refrigerator door or bulletin board are the collage that paints a picture of your daily life. What's on yours and why?

Go digging in your wallet or handbag for receipts and scraps of paper. What do they say about you and your world?

_____

_____

How much did you pay for gas? _____

What are people saying about oil and other sources of fuel? _____

_____

Tell about the last item you returned to the store. _____

_____

_____

_____

If you've gotten a library fine, what book were you reading and why were you late?

_____

_____

Write average prices for common items:

Bread _____

Milk _____

Eggs _____

Gas _____

Soap _____

Car _____

Two-bedroom house _____

· TIME CAPSULE ·

Use these two pages to make out your usual "to do" lists. If your kind of list usually consists of groceries and a meal plan, write that down. If you have been working on a list of goals or a list for holiday gifts, use that. Or use a few. These lists create a snapshot of your daily life.

ALL ABOUT ME

· TIME MARKERS ·

What are the three most dramatic and historically significant events during your lifetime? (Martin Luther King, Jr. assassinated, destruction of the Berlin Wall, collapse of the Soviet Union, the moon landing, the Vietnam War, the Twin Towers toppling?)

1. ....

2. ....

3. ....

Who were you with when these historic events happened? What was it like for you? What was it like for your parents, grandparents, and/or children?

....

....

....

....

....

....

....

....

....

What other historic events have made an impression on you and those close to you?

· RIGHT NOW ·

Who is president/prime minister? ....

What political issues are most pressing domestically? ....

_____

_____

_____

_____

_____

_____

What political issues are most pressing internationally? ....

_____

_____

_____

_____

_____

_____

ALL ABOUT ME

Who are the hottest stars in:

film? ....

theater? ....

television? ....

music? ....

What news is big in the tabloids? ....

....

....

Describe the latest technology and trends in:

Computers ....

....

....

The Internet ....

....

....

Television ....

....

....

Sound ....

....

....

· BODY PARTS ·

How about your:

- feet

- nose

- lips

- hair

- eyes

- nails

- legs

What's the last time you did something nice for your body?

o you appreciate your body or are you critical? How so?

o you get regular physicals?

re you neglecting any part of your physical health? *(Explain.)*

re you especially diligent at tending to particular health issues?

· GET READY, GET SET, GET HEALTHY ·

Here's the skinny on journaling. Recording everything you eat and drink, how much, and when, even without a specific diet plan, is a very effective way to reach your ideal weight. Ditto for exercise. Note everything you eat and your level of activity for one day.

	Morning	Afternoon	Evening
Food/drink consumed			
Exercise			

Did you eat out of physical hunger alone? *(Explain.)*

id you notice any unconscious eating? *(Explain.)* ....

....

....

....

. what ways did you avoid opportunities to exert yourself—like taking the elevator or
.rking as close to the entrance as possible at the grocery store—or not?

....

....

....

.fe coach Martha Beck swears that being fit depends largely on how much non-caloric joy you can
.eate. Make a list of the zero calorie activities that bring you pleasure.

....

....

....

....

....

....

.ep going.

....

....

....

....

· TWENTY-FOUR KARATS ·

Today choose more carrots than sticks. Be kind to yourself. Take time to savor your achievements. Remembering all that you have done and can do will boost your confidence and oomph for success.

List twenty-four things, big or small, that you've done right. Include anything that was successful, challenging, kind, new, or good.

for the gold and keep writing. Continue to write down your accomplishments each day. It will ease your path to success and that ride will be faster and a lot more fun.

· AM I MY MOTHER OR FATHER? ·

Do you ever look into the mirror and see your parents? In what way(s)?

_____

_____

_____

_____

_____

Do you ever hear their words tumbling from your lips? Which ones?

_____

_____

_____

_____

_____

Were you nagged, lectured, or overprotected in your youth, and if so, how?

_____

_____

_____

_____

_____

ow are you (or will you be) different with your own kids?

....

....

....

....

e you a better (or worse) spouse and parent, and in what ways?

....

....

....

....

r has it seemed (as Mark Twain once suggested) that your parents just keep getting smarter as you
ature? What traits of your parents do you appreciate now that you're older?

....

....

....

....

id you at some point switch roles to become the caretaker of your parents? If so, how? If not,
scribe their lifestyle.

....

....

....

· ME-ZILLA ·

Have you ever been completely out of control? How?

If you've ever acted selfish, egotistical, or ruthless, what pushed you to that point?

Describe a time when you were secretly (or overtly) pleased at another's misfortune.

Describe a case of road rage or a temper tantrum.

Write about a time when you screamed at the top of your lungs, or ripped someone apart with words. *(If you've never misbehaved, why not?)*

What are your triggers or your pet peeves?

· ZIPLOCK YOUR MEMORY ·

We usually rely on sight and sound to remember things. But if you anchor a memory to smell, touch, or taste it can stay fresh indefinitely. A memory that links to an emotional state is even further protected against loss. Write about this very moment, or a recent experience, and include as much sensory detail as possible.

ALL ABOUT ME

Write about a memory tied to a:

Smell

Taste

Sight

Touch

Sound

Good feeling

Bad feeling

ALL ABOUT ME

· A RETROSPECTIVE ·

How old are you now? ....

What is the best age to be? ....

....

What was the best year in your life, and why? ....

....

....

The worst? Why? ....

....

....

How do you feel about getting older? ....

....

....

What did you wonder about when you were younger? ....

....

....

Do you still think about those things? What do you wonder now? ....

....

....

ALL ABOUT ME

What did you do when you were younger that you can't do now?

What can you do now that you couldn't do then?

What are you most looking forward to at this stage of life?

What are the 10 things you most want to be sure to see, do, or accomplish before you die?

What are your favorite things to do now?

· THE END ·

What was your first experience dealing with death? *(pet, grandparent, other)*

Do you believe in heaven, hell, or reincarnation? What do those things mean to you?

What do you think will happen after you die?

Would you prefer to be buried (where?) or cremated?

How would you like to be remembered?

Write the obituary or eulogy you'd like to have.

Now, can you live up to it?

ALL ABOUT ME

· NOTES TO SELF ·

ALL ABOUT ME

• NOTES TO SELF •

· NOTES TO SELF ·

THE INNER ME

How can I guess what I know before I say it?

—HANNAH FELDSPAR

These pages provide the place for serious and playful introspection. Your answers will reveal much about who you are—to yourself and to any you share with. There is room here for revelation, imagination, opining, telling secrets, fantasizing, boasting, complaining, and setting down memories of life-changing events. Your responses may bring insight and clarity, proving that, as John Fowles writes, "The most important questions in life can never be answered by anyone except oneself."

I never travel without my diary.
One should always have
something sensational to read in the train.

—OSCAR WILDE

· IDEOLOGY ·

What core values define you? *(What personal beliefs have affected the way you think, act, or understand the world?)*

_____

_____

_____

_____

_____

How well have you been able to balance:

• Your personal life with work life? _____

_____

_____

• Others' needs with your own? _____

_____

_____

• Self-acceptance with critical self-evaluation? _____

_____

_____

THE INNER ME

Describe the best day in your life so far.

How about the best day that hasn't happened—yet!

If you had no personal ties or obligations, where would you choose to live?

What kind of partner would you have and how would you spend your time?

· SELF MATTERS ·

To be your own best critic, ask yourself some questions.

What health concerns do I need to address? ....

....

....

....

What needs fixing in my life? *(car, roof, lock, tooth?)* ....

....

....

How could I create more energy? *(exercise, get more sleep?)* ....

....

....

What needs replacing? *(babysitter, computer, hairstyle, job?)* ....

....

....

What do I need to get started on *(the gardening, my taxes?)* before it gets out of hand?

....

....

THE INNER ME

should stop: ....

....

....

would be better off without: ....

....

need more: ....

....

....

need less: ....

....

....

should spend more time with: ....

....

t's about time I: ....

....

....

need to give myself: ....

....

What else do I want to ask myself? ....

....

....

· PERSONAL TRIVIA ·

What odd facts do you remember that most everyone else doesn't?

What in all creation awes you most?

What law or rule would you most like to see created or enforced?

Are there any little red circles with slash signs that you'd like to add to the ever present
NO SMOKING, NO PETS, NO TRESPASSING signs?

Any you'd like to tear down? Why?

Did you ever fail at something after you gave it everything you had, and what was it?

Under what circumstances would you try again?

What foreign languages have you tried to learn?

If you could be instantly fluent, what new language would you like to speak?

THE INNER ME

What one tourist attraction should everyone try to see at least once? ....

....

What six places would you like to visit in your lifetime?

....

....

....

What hobby could be your full-time job—if only it paid? ....

....

Whose sports prowess would you like to possess? ....

Do you have any irrational fear? What is it? ....

....

....

If you know it is irrational, why do you think you still have the fear? ....

....

....

In what ways are you brave? ....

....

How did you get involved in something that you were sorry for? Or were you sorry that you didn't get more involved?

....

....

....

· MUSIC ·

What kind of music do you enjoy most often?

What are a few of your favorite songs?

Do you play an instrument or sing in a group? Did you ever? *(Describe.)*

Do you whistle? *(Descibe your style).*

Do you like to dance?

How often do you have an opportunity to dance?

How would you describe your dance style?

What was your most memorable dance?

t a party would you tend to sit out the fast dances or the slow ones? ....

....

o you ever dance by yourself? If so, describe the circumstances. ....

....

hose famous singing voice or other great talent would you love to have?

....

....

las the same old jingle from an ad or song ever played itself over and over in your head?

....

....

an you name that tune? ....

....

....

; there a piece of music that always makes you remember a certain event? *(Describe.)*

....

....

....

....

· MIND OVER MATTER ·

For you, how much is physical and how much is mental in each of these situations? Explain:

• Having the edge in a sport or some other physical challenge

• Falling in love

• Feeling tired

• Getting a headache

• Craving sweets

• Needing physical affection

· RIDE A CAMEL ·

What are some things you have done that most other people have not?

_____

_____

_____

· TIME ·

What urgent but not very important activities eat up your time? _____

_____

_____

What important but not at all urgent tasks do you usually put off? _____

_____

_____

What are three IMPORTANT THINGS that you can do in ten minutes? _____

_____

_____

What unpleasant task can you tolerate if you do it for only fifteen minutes at a time?

_____

_____

· DID YOU EVER? ·

Did you ever? (or if not, would you?) Give details.

• Steal something

• Pose for a nude drawing or photograph

• Go to the emergency room

• Tell off a teacher, boss, or some other authority figure

• Skip a grade

• Flunk a class

• Laugh inappropriately at a wedding or funeral

• Appear on TV

• Eat something that has fallen onto the floor

THE INNER ME

Pretend you were someone else *(in person? on the phone?)* ....

Hitchhike ....

Skinny dip ....

Pray for a miracle ....

Witness a miracle ....

Ride a roller coaster ....

Break a bone ....

Bungee jump ....

Shoot a gun ....

Risk your safety to save someone in peril ....

Join a fraternity, sorority, or other club ....

· HIGH TIMES ·

How close have you come to heaven? *(Been on a roof, up a tree, in a hot air balloon, close to death, in an altered state of consciousness, had a moment of pure ecstasy?)* Describe in detail.

Under what conditions would you travel to outer space?

· ONE BIG STICK ·

Sometimes the expectation of pleasure doesn't create enough momentum to make us do what we need to have what we want. Pick out one (only one!) thing you'd like to change about yourself and write convincingly about how not doing something about that one thing holds you back and hurts you or the people you love.

· GET OVER YOURSELF—BE SOMEONE ELSE ·

> Stumped? Has some stubborn problem suddenly popped its ugly head into your life? Think of someone you admire. Someone who would tackle your issue bravely with intelligence and grace. Pick anyone. Ben Franklin, your gutsy neighbor, your coach, Maya Angelou, the Dalai Lama, or Oprah. What would any one of them do? Pretend you are that person and write down their advice to you. Make it a team effort. Let them all have a say.

If I were

I wouldn't let

hold me back at all. I would just

If I were

I wouldn't let

hold me back at all. I would just

· OWN WHAT YOU KNOW ·

Got a tough decision to make? Not sure about how to handle a problem? Put your dilemma on the page.

....

....

....

....

....

Now call upon your higher self, your intuition, or your source of inspiration and start writing. Don't think too hard.

....

....

....

....

....

....

....

....

Now read it aloud. Did you tap into any unexpected wisdom? ....

....

....

· JOY ·

Stop and think about everything you have and love in your life at this very moment.

What brings you happiness? *(the fine hair on your lover's neck, your child's smile, the sun streaming through your window, the smell of lilacs?)*

How much room do you have in your heart for happiness?

What can you be happy about right now?

What do you risk when you allow yourself to experience pleasure?

· HOLY CARP ·

There is nothing fishy about putting your complaints on paper. Paying attention to them is one of the best ways to get clear about what you want. List what you hate in Column A. Now, in Column B, rephrase each negative statement with its opposite. Be specific. (Change "I hate my meaningless job" to "I want to work in a children's hospital and get paid well for it.") Notice how Column A feels static while Column B implies action? After you are finished with your list draw a big black X through Column A and start thinking about small but immediate steps you can take toward making Column B your reality.

Column A (what I hate):

Column B (what I want):

In Chinese mythology, Dragon's Gate is a magic place at the top of a waterfall. The carp that can rise high enough from the water below to jump through it will become a beautiful dragon. So keep carping until you rise above your unhappy circumstances.

· ONE-WORD PROMPTS ·

Even one-word prompts can rev up your thinking and stir up an insight. Write quickly and don't second-guess yourself.

When do you feel:

Adored

Afraid

Ambitious

Angry

Ashamed

Bored

Cocky

Confused

Content

Courageous

Cruel

Disappointed

Embarrassed

Exhausted

Grateful

Greedy

THE INNER ME

Guilty

Happy

Inspired

Intimidated

Jealous

Left out

Lonely

Needed

Obsessed

Passionate

Proud

Relieved

Remorseful

Resentful

Selfish

Sensuous

Stressed

Sympathetic

Threatened

Trusted

Vengeful

Circle those responses that felt most true.

· MY DARK SIDE ·

Some say we all have a double. Have you ever met someone who looks just like you?

....

....

If you could be cloned, would you do it? ....

....

Assuming you get to experience everything your clone does, what is the most extreme lifestyle, look, job, or mission you would direct it to undertake?

....

....

....

....

....

The *doppelgänger* is your mythological evil twin, kind of your dark side impersonated. What would you *doppelgänger* be like?

....

....

....

....

....

EVERYTHING YOU WANT TO KNOW ABOUT YOURSELF BUT WERE AFRAID TO ASK

Call someone who knew you as a kid and ask them what you were like. What did you find out?

Ask someone who knows you well and sees you often what your strengths and weaknesses are. Who did you ask and what did you learn about yourself?

What did they say that you agree or disagree with?

THE INNER ME

· YIN YANG ·

What are your opinions about:

- Smoking

- Dessert

- Being prompt

- Yourself

- Your spouse or closest friend

- Correct grammar

- Housekeeping

- Your exercise routine

- Drinking

- Going green *(making environmentally safe choices)*

- War

• UP CLOSE AND PERSONAL •

A change in perspective is worth 80 IQ points.

—ALAN KAY

If you could rerun three moments from your life what would they be?

_____

_____

_____

_____

_____

_____

_____

_____

_____

_____

Did you choose those moments to relive pleasure, to learn something about your past, or to get it right the second time around?

_____

_____

_____

_____

· BACK TO THE FUTURE ·

If you could fast-forward life to see what will happen a few years from now, would you do it?

What would you want to know?

What would you not want to know?

· POSTHUMOUSLY SPEAKING ·

Write a letter to your great-great-grandchild or to another child of the future. Speculate about what the planet will be like by then. Use your imagination. What medical and technological advances will have been developed? What are your hopes and fears for future generations?

· ME, MYSELF, AND I ·

If a movie were to be made about your life, who would play you?

What would the title be?

What music would be in the sound track?

What type of movie would it be? *(thriller, comedy, tearjerker)*

Do you star in your own life?

If not, who does, and why?

Who would you cast as spouse, best friend, parents, boss, other?

....

....

....

....

In real life who plays the supporting role, the director, the extra?

....

....

....

....

Does your movie have a happy ending? *(Explain.)* ....

....

....

....

Would you change the plot? If so, how? ....

....

....

....

....

· REPRIEVE ·

You get to come back to life for just long enough to say good-bye, convey your feelings, or give a few words of advice. What do you decide to say and to whom?

· ENCORE ·

Einstein, Ben Franklin, Napoleon, and Mark Twain believed in reincarnation. Do you?

Imagine scientists reconstitute your DNA into a brand-new you. You are the same old protoplasm but with an opportunity for a fresh start. What do you want to do this time around?

If you were given the opportunity to be reborn with any kind of body, mind, and life circumstance, would you choose that instead?

Who would you want to be?

· MIRROR, MIRROR ·

What is your true nature? ....

....

....

Who are you when you are not being what you do for a living, or fulfilling the role(s) of friend, parent, or spouse?

....

....

....

....

....

....

Answer this question: Who am I? ....

....

....

Now answer it in another way. ....

....

Again. ....

....

And again. ....

....

nswer it at least 20 times until you have exhausted all of the roles you normally play.

· GRATITUDE ·

When you take time to notice and appreciate the present moment you experience life more fully. Those who make a daily practice of noting the big and small things for which they are grateful claim that doing so kick-starts an attraction for even greater abundance. Name ten things for which you feel grateful. Elaborate.

1. ....

....

....

2. ....

....

....

3. ....

....

....

4. ....

....

....

5. ....

....

....

dd more as you're inspired to do so.

THE INNER ME

· NOTES TO SELF ·

WHAT NEXT?

Write down the thoughts of the moment. Those that come unsought for are commonly the most valuable.

—FRANCIS BACON

Congratulations on completing your journal entries. You have just produced a book so unique that only you could have written it. You have recorded the rudiments of a family history, given expression to your inner voice, encouraged your creative muses and hopefully had some fun. Memories trigger memories and questions provoke questions, so you may well find that you suddenly have a lot more to say. The more you examine your personal history and inner thoughts the more meaningful and life changing that process can become.

Journals are often cited as tools for change. People claim that they have coaxed both more abundance and pleasant synchronicities into their lives by writing about gratitude and their clear intentions. Julia Cameron says that writing done first thing in the morning both primes the pump to clear your head, and forces you to drag reality out for inspection. Maybe writing is a type of moving meditation. Perhaps we all have important knowledge and right answers inside that we just don't pay attention to. Journaling is one way to value our own intuition and to own what we already know. Maybe there really is some magic in putting pen to paper.

If you feel encouraged to do some free writing, here are exercises that can help ease you onto the blank page and slip you past the dreaded writer's block.

· WRITING FLUID ·

The only questions that really matter are the ones you ask yourself.

—URSULA K. LE GUINN

Be your own investigative interviewer and invent your own series of questions. When you were a child you probably asked "why?" often and with abandon. Without censoring yourself, write down every deep, silly, commonplace, provocative, and outrageous question that comes to mind. And then answer them as sincerely as possible. See if your subconscious mind doesn't catch your critical mind off guard to yield some surprising and revealing insights.

Use the next eight pages for fluid writing.

WHAT NEXT?

WHAT NEXT?

WHAT NEXT?

WHAT NEXT?

WHAT NEXT?

WHAT NEXT?

· PROPRIOCEPTION ·

It always comes back to the same necessity: go deep enough and there is a bedrock of truth, however hard.

—MAY SARTON

When you can't think of anything to say, trick yourself. Here is a quick start course in the highly effective Proprioceptive (PRO-pree-o-SEP-tiv) writing technique. There are whole books and seminars on how to use your "Muscle-sense" (stimulation from movement, effort, stretch, and the relative position of one body part to another) to tap into your forgotten memories, deepest emotions, and spontaneous creativity. Or you can just follow these directions to get the gist of it.

Sit comfortably and light a candle to create an atmosphere of pleasant expectation and ritual. Put on some baroque music (Bach, Scarlatti, Vivaldi, or your personal preference) to rouse the favored brain waves and get started. Don't worry about choosing a topic. Just record every sensation and random thought as it occurs to you without pausing. No stopping, judging, or even lifting your hand from the page allowed! If you can't think of anything to say, just write the words "I can't think of anything to say," and keep going. Each time you feel stuck, refer to your last sentence and keep going, or write the words "What do I mean by that?"

Let the music and the physical sensations produced in your body as your hand slides across the page have their way with you. Many accomplished writers use this technique to overcome writer's block. Try it and you may be surprised by the topics that crawl up your spine and onto the page.

Use the next six pages for proprioceptive writing.

WHAT NEXT?

WHAT NEXT?

WHAT NEXT?

WHAT NEXT?

WHAT NEXT?

WHAT NEXT?

WHAT NEXT?

· RANDOM INSPIRATION ·

I didn't really say half the things I said.

—YOGI BERRA

Stichomancy is an ancient form of divination in which a random passage from a book believed to hold the truth is used to give guidance or hint at the future. Close your eyes and open any book (preferably one that you believe holds wisdom [e.g., the Bible, the I Ching, or a book about runes]) to any page. Point and then write down the ways you think that selection could apply to you.

Use the work you just did as a foundation. Go back and read what you have written. What new details occur to you? Write in the margins. *(He later became a Marine and she got pregnant and dropped out of tenth grade. He helped crazy Sherry paint her house Revlon Red. On second thought, I hate . . .)*

If you have a lot to say about something or someone, grab some blank pages and write about it until you feel finished.

Be playful, try to enjoy the process of writing, and don't underestimate the value of what you have to say. Write as you speak—conversationally. Don't let yourself get discouraged and never give up. You can't be too young (Anne Frank was 13) nor too old (published author Sadie Delany was 109) to create a treasure for yourself, your family, and for many generations to come.

Use the next five pages to record random inspirations.

WHAT NEXT?

WHAT NEXT?

WHAT NEXT?

WHAT NEXT?

WHAT NEXT?